So you really want to learn

Geography

Book Two
Answer Book

James Dale-Adcock

Series Editor: Simon Lewis

GALORE PARK

www.galorepark.co.uk

Published by Galore Park Publishing Ltd
19/21 Sayers Lane, Tenterden, Kent TN30 6BW

www.galorepark.co.uk

Text copyright © James Dale-Adcock 2007

Typography by Typetechnique, London
Printed and bound by CPI Antony Rowe, Chippenham

ISBN-13: 978 1 905735 28 0

First published 2007, reprinted 2008

Details of other Galore Park publications are available at
www.galorepark.co.uk

ISEB Revision Guides, publications and examination papers may also be
obtained from Galore Park.

Contents

Introduction

The answers provided by this answer book are by no means prescriptive. Some topics, such as Location knowledge or Mapwork, lend themselves to specific 'right' or 'wrong' answers, however, many areas of Geography are subjective, and a range of answers are feasible if sound reasoning is given. Although it is not always practical, marking with the pupil present is good practice and can be a method of shared learning for the teacher or parent and child, as well as a perfect opportunity for reward.

If a pupil provides an answer not given in this book it is always wise to ask them how they came to their conclusion. This may be more pertinent to the answers for Level 2 activities, which are designed to challenge more able pupils and scholarship candidates and which, by their nature, may elicit a wider range of responses. For these questions, the key points to be covered are given. These may then be elaborated upon in different ways.

James Dale-Adcock
2007

Chapter 1: Mapwork

Exercise 1A

1. (a) Multiple answers possible, e.g.: public house
   (b) Multiple answers possible, e.g.: mixed wood
   (c) Multiple answers possible, e.g.: (permitted) bridleway
   (d) Multiple answers possible, e.g.: telephone box

2. (a) Five answers from the following possible references:

486008	494995	491989
484005	497996	495988
484995	499999	502992
487987	490002	

   (b) 486008:   north-west
       484005:   north-west
       484995:   west
       487987:   south-west
       494995:   east/north-east
       497996:   east/north-east
       499999:   north-east
       490002:   north/north-west
       490989:   south/south-west
       495988:   south
       502992:   east/south-east

3. (a) train driver
   (b) golf professional
   (c) farmer
   (d) museum curator

4. (a) 8 kilometres
   (b) 10 kilometres

5. Steep-sided valleys to north-east of park (tightly packed contour lines).
   High point of 106 metres (triangulation pillar in grid square 0109).
   Gentle slopes to south-west of park (well spaced contour lines).

Exercise 1B

1. 010057   998081   018092   066094

2. (a) valley
   (b) ridge
   (c) round top hill
   (d) gentle slope

3. 4.5 square kilometres

4. The relief in the north-east is steep and variable with many features such as round top hills (081101), valleys (055115), ridges (070090) and tightly packed contour lines (054095) with a maximum height of 141 metres (triangulation point in grid square 0609).

   Whereas the relief in the south-west has very gentle slopes (995063) and flat land (002042).

5. Pupils should have drawn a sketch section like the one shown below. It should include the following features: streams, footpaths, roads less than 4m wide.

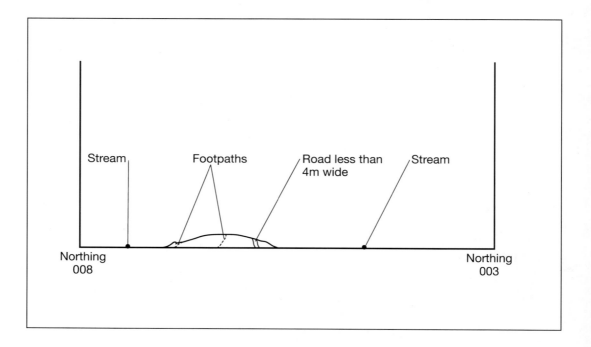

Exercise 1C

1. (a) golf course
   (b) post office
   (c) (permitted) bridleway

2. Any one of the following grid references:
   5480   5783   5782   5781

3. Multiple answers possible, for example:
   - information centre in Castleton (149831)
   - caravan/campsites at various locations
   - youth hostel in Castleton (149828)

4. Multiple answers possible, for example:
   - physical features: River Noe and valley sides
   - human features: college and quarry

Exercise 1D

1. Multiple answers possible, for example:

parking, park and ride:	575777	573787
golf course or links:	546777	
telephone, public/motoring organisation:	583801	551815
camp site/caravan site:	575819	570833
post office:	529818	548798
public house:	548799	530815
National Park:	none on map	
National Trust:	581796	562782
footpath:	535785	552786
bridleway:	535784	557818

2. Pupils may describe various routes for their journey on foot between Bradwell and Castleton. One option, walking along the minor roads, may be described as follows:

Take the B6049 north out of Bradwell. At grid reference 174818 take a left onto a minor road heading towards Hope. You will come to a T-junction just before Hope, turn left here and follow the road to Castleton. Alternatively, continue into Hope and turn left on the A6187 and follow this road to Castleton.

Examples of physical features passed: non-coniferous trees / Bradwell Brook.

Examples of human features passed: sewage works / railway line.

Pupils may decide on a walk that takes them along the unclassified road north-west out of Bradwell (branching off left from the B6049). When you meet the T-junction take the footpath towards Pindale Farm. You will pass the following features:

Physical features passed: non-coniferous trees; human features: pub in Bradwell, quarry, disused mine shafts, works, chimney, campsite.

Once you reach Pindale Farm you will join another unclassified road. Follow the road north-east past Pin Dale (physical feature) towards Castleton. You will pass more physical features such as a wood with non-coniferous trees, a cliff top and human features such as the remains of Peveril Castle.

Exercise 1E

1. In the future this part of the river will become an ox-bow lake.

2. The flat land that is either side of the River Clyst is called the floodplain.

    There are no buildings on this land because of the risk of flooding.

    The land could be used for farming because the silt deposited during floods can make the soil very fertile.

3. The night-time temperatures are likely to be several degrees warmer in 9392 because the high density of housing in the city radiates more heat.

4. The south-facing slope of Pyne's Hill means the school receives afternoon sunshine, which indicates that the temperature reading might be higher than elsewhere.

    Shade, prevailing wind direction, surface and physical features could also influence how warm or cold it is at a school.

5. Bishop's Court in grid square 9891 is a hamlet because it is small and has no services.

6. Multiple answers are possible, for example:

    You might site a supermarket at grid reference 956907 because:
    • the land is relatively flat for building on
    • it is close to a major roundabout giving good access
    • it is near the urban market of Exeter

7.   East of easting 97 is a well-drained area. The reason for this is that there are many overland channels, streams and the River Clyst. There is also significant gradient causing westerly drainage into the River Clyst.

Exercise 1F

1.   Groynes are designed to stop longshore drift. Longshore drift is the movement of sand and stones/pebbles along a beach in a zigzag fashion in the direction of the prevailing wind.

2.   The types of coastal erosion that we see at Luccombe Bay and Horse Ledge in grid squares 5879 and 5880 have depended on the resistance of the rock. Horse Ledge could be made of resistant rock and Luccombe Bay of less resistant rock. The hydraulic action of waves and abrasion has worn the rocks away at different rates.

3.   During the winter months, the rock that forms Shanklin Down will be subject to freeze-thaw weathering if temperatures range either side of freezing. Its exposed position means it will certainly receive sufficient rainfall to aid freeze-thaw weathering. Shanklin Down is also partially covered by vegetation and will therefore experience biological weathering. The area may also be subject to chemical weathering depending on the rock type, although this is indiscernible from the map.

4.   Multiple answers are possible, for example:

You might build a weather station at grid reference 157830 because this site is on flat land; it is not influenced by buildings but is close to a footpath to allow easy access.

5.   Multiple answers are possible, for example:

Primary industry:	Wroxall Manor Farm (559791)
	Bigbury Farm (567835)
	Week Farm (536779)

Tertiary industry:	model village (527817)
	public house (548799)
	information centre (581813)

6. (a) Shanklin and Ventnor on the Isle of Wight are both linear settlements.

    (b) They are linear settlements because they have been built along the coastline.

    (c) Multiple answers are possible, for example:
    - Godshill (5282) is a nucleated settlement
    - Summersbury (5482) is a dispersed settlement

7. There are a number of examples that show how different industries are placing pressure on the Peak District:
    - tourism in the form of camp/caravan sites (1882) causes visual pollution
    - works (1682) could cause noise, air or visual pollution
    - disused mines (1481) could cause visual pollution and be an environmental hazard

    Industries placing pressure on the environment on the Isle of Wight:
    - tourism: parking areas (5778), camp/caravan sites (5782), airport (5783), picnic areas (5879) cause visual and noise pollution
    - telecommunications: masts (5678) cause visual pollution

Exercise 1G: Enquiry suggestion
Practical

Exercise 1H: Past exam questions

1. 149828: youth hostel
    153810: disused mine

2. The River Noe flows towards the south-east. We know this from the map because of the direction of tributaries and the reduced height of land towards the south-east shown by the spot heights.

3. The distance by road from the junction at Goose Hill (144828) to the church at Hope (172835) is 3 kilometres.

4. Both the mining area (1481) now used as farmland (evidence cattle grids 1481) and the camping and caravan sites on farmland (1583) are evidence of change in land use west of easting 16.

Exercise 1I: Mapwork summary crossword

Answers across:
1. Cartographer
2. Triangulation
3. Key
4. Plateau

Answers down:
1. Bearings
2. Relief
3. Gradient
4. Spot height
5. Easting

Chapter 2: Landform processes

Exercise 2A

1. Weathering is the breakdown of rock by the weather in one place.
   Erosion is the wearing away and movement of rock by a force (wind, sea, rivers, etc.)

2. Transportation is the movement of a river's load downstream.
   Load is the material carried by a river.
   The channel is the bed and banks of a river within which the water flows.

3. Physical or mechanical: Freeze-thaw weathering

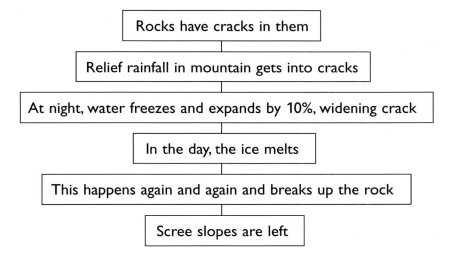

Physical or mechanical: Onion-skin weathering

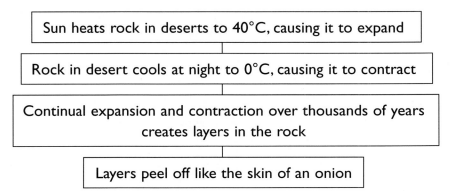

Chemical weathering

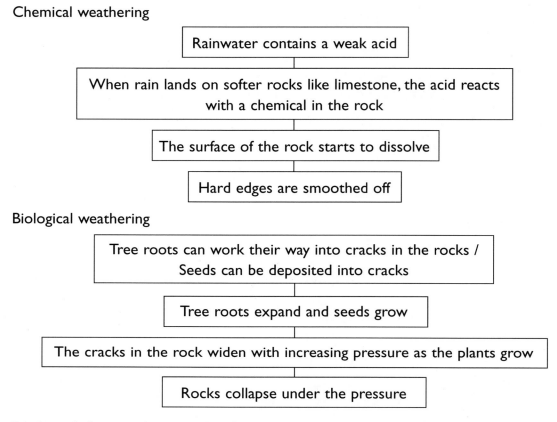

Rainwater contains a weak acid

When rain lands on softer rocks like limestone, the acid reacts with a chemical in the rock

The surface of the rock starts to dissolve

Hard edges are smoothed off

Biological weathering

Tree roots can work their way into cracks in the rocks / Seeds can be deposited into cracks

Tree roots expand and seeds grow

The cracks in the rock widen with increasing pressure as the plants grow

Rocks collapse under the pressure

Pupils may also use the example of animals burrowing and causing the rocks to collapse.

4. Pupils are required to draw a labelled diagram showing any two of the processes of erosion. The diagrams should have a title, be labelled correctly and there should be a sentence underneath saying where the process is likely to occur in the course of a river.

    A diagram to show how hydraulic action causes erosion

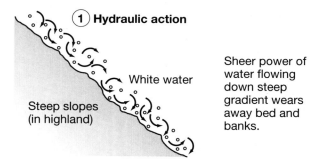

① **Hydraulic action**

White water

Steep slopes (in highland)

Sheer power of water flowing down steep gradient wears away bed and banks.

Hydraulic action is most likely to be significant in highland when the water is flowing fast down a steep gradient.

A diagram to show how abrasion causes erosion

(2) **Abrasion**

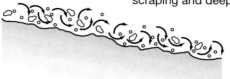

River's load bounces along the bottom of the channel, scraping and deepening it.

Abrasion will be more significant in highland when the river is flowing fast down a steep gradient.

A diagram to show how corrosion causes erosion

(3) **Corrosion**

River could flow over rock that can be gradually dissolved (e.g. limestone).

Corrosion may occur in any part of the river's course depending upon which type of rock the river is flowing over.

A diagram to show how attrition causes erosion

(4) **Attrition**

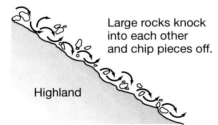

Large rocks knock into each other and chip pieces off.

The load becomes smaller and rounder as it reaches lowland.

Highland

Lowland

Attrition may occur in any part of the river's course.

Exercise 2B

1. Pupils may give the following types of answers:

    Evidence of chemical weathering: crumbling stonework.

    Evidence of biological weathering: paving stones being lifted; tarmac cracking as tree roots expand and cause surface to crack; animal burrows causing rocks to collapse (if your school or home is near a rocky area!).

2. A river's load changes shape by the time it reaches its lower course. In highland the river's load will be sharp, large and angular because it is made of weathered material from the valley sides and has not been in the river long enough to be eroded.

    As the load is transported downstream by **saltation**, and possibly **traction** in times of flood, it will rub and collide against itself causing it to break into smaller particles, a process called **attrition**. As the load is carried further downstream the pebbles become smoother and rounder and erode the river channel, a process called **abrasion**. These processes will gradually make the load smaller and rounder by the time the river begins to deposit its load in lowland on the inside of meanders and finally to form the delta.

3. **Abrasion** and **saltation** often occur when the river is flowing down a steep gradient. The river's load erodes the channel bed and banks by abrasion and the small pieces of eroded rock are moved downstream by saltation at the same time.

    Hydraulic action and **traction** often occur when the river is flowing down a steep gradient in highland. The river's power erodes the channel bed and banks by hydraulic action and the pieces of eroded rock are moved downstream by traction at the same time.

    Corrosion and **solution** always act in tandem. River water contains a small degree of natural acid within it that may erode the rock that forms the channel by corrosion. The dissolved rock is then carried away within the river water as solution.

4. **Temperature** is an important factor in weathering. A European mountain range such as the Alps will experience a high number of occasions when the temperature range varies either side of freezing. This permits the processes of freeze-thaw weathering to take place. The Himalayas, surprisingly, experience less freeze-thaw weathering because the temperature rarely rises above freezing, certainly on the higher slopes.

Freeze-thaw weathering requires moisture as well as a temperature range either side of zero; therefore **precipitation** levels are also a contributing factor in the speed of this type of weathering. For example, the night-time temperature in a desert such as the Sahara may well fall below freezing but the lack of moisture will prevent freeze-thaw weathering from taking place.

Both chemical weathering and biological weathering are accelerated with increased temperature and precipitation levels. Tropical and Equatorial regions will therefore experience significant biological weathering and could experience chemical weathering depending on the **rock type**. Areas that are composed of rocks such as limestone, which are likely to be dissolved by weak acid in rainwater, will experience high levels of chemical weathering such as the Malham area of North Yorkshire.

Exercise 2C

1. **A river basin** is the area of land that is drained by a river.

   A watershed is the dividing line between two or more river basins.

   Vertical erosion is erosion downwards into the rock, and occurs in highland due to the steep gradient.

   Lateral erosion is erosion from side to side, and occurs in lowland due to the gentle gradient.

2. (a) The three processes that lead to the formation of a V-shaped valley are erosion, weathering and transportation.

   (b) The stages of formation of a V-shaped valley:

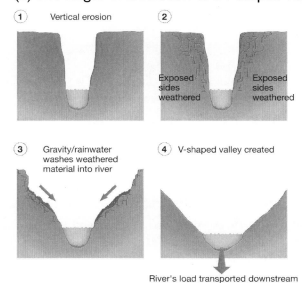

River's load transported downstream

3. A flow chart showing the stages in the formation of a waterfall.

> Rivers may flow over rock bands of different resistance in highland.

> Hydraulic action and abrasion will wear down the less resistant rock faster than the resistant rock, creating a step in the river.

> In time the step will lead to the water flowing down onto the less resistant rock, which will create a plunge pool. The plunge pool will be deepened by abrasion and hydraulic action.

> Spray created from water falling into the plunge pool will settle on the back wall of the waterfall, undercutting it by chemical weathering.

> This will cause an overhang of the resistant rock, which will eventually give way and collapse into the plunge pool. In time, this material will be broken up and moved downstream by transportation.

> Repetition of this process will cause the whole waterfall to move back towards its source, leaving behind a steep-sided valley called a gorge.

4. (a) A floodplain is the flat land either side of a river which is rich in fertile soil.

(b) We may well find ox-bow lakes on floodplains for the following reasons. As a river moves into lowland it flows over a more gentle **gradient**. The river's power begins to erode from side to side rather than just downwards, a process called **lateral erosion**. Lateral erosion causes meanders, which become more **sinuous** as the river approaches the sea.

When the **necks** of meanders become very narrow the river water skips over the **neck** and follows the easiest path, thereby cutting off the meander. This cut-off meander is known as an ox-bow lake. As soon as the main flow of the river is not travelling through the ox-bow lake it becomes stagnant and the remaining **load** will be **deposited**. Evaporation of the water in the lake will follow and, over time, the redundant meander, the ox-bow lake, will be **invaded by plant life**. Plant life will **photosynthesise** and continue to take over the meander.

Exercise 2D

1. source   tributary   estuary   delta

2. Leck Beck is flowing through highland over a steeper gradient than the River Greta. This means that Leck Beck will be eroding vertically and therefore flows in a relatively straight line. River Greta, however, has begun to meander, eroding laterally as it flows over a more gentle gradient in lower land.

3. Check pupils' research on the waterfall of their choice. Ensure they have used their own words and have applied what they have learned about waterfalls in their answer. The answer should include half a page of information about the waterfall chosen, the country the waterfall is in and any interesting facts.

4. A waterfall is formed when there is a difference in the height of the land over which a river flows. This difference may have been caused by the movement of the earth's plates or because a glacier has deepened a valley leaving tributaries hanging above their confluences. One of the most common causes of waterfalls is a river flowing over rock types of different resistance (e.g. Niagara Falls).

    As a waterfall retreats towards its source it leaves behind it a very steep-sided valley called a gorge. The Niagara Gorge is 11 kilometres long. However, a gorge can also be created when underground caverns created by corrosion within limestone collapse such as Gordale in the Malham area of North Yorkshire.

Exercise 2E

1. Along some points of the coastline we can see bays appearing between headlands. This is because in these parts of the coastline there are different bands of rock with different levels of resistance.

    Resistant rock, such as granite will be eroded at a slower rate than surrounding less resistant rock such as limestone, sandstone or chalk. Headlands are created from the hard rock, which has taken longer to erode than the surrounding softer rock. Where the softer rock is worn away between the headlands, bays are created.

2. Check pupils have drawn a sketch like the one below:

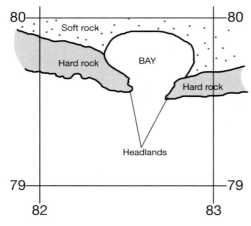

3. **Headlands**, which are formed from **resistant rock** can receive the full force of all four types of erosion as they protrude out into the sea. As the **prevailing wind** direction faces the **headland** side on, **abrasion** will widen **cracks** at the base of the headland, while **hydraulic action** from the waves will widen the **crack** higher up. Over time a **crack** will be widened to create a sea **cave**, which in turn will erode through the **headland** to create an arch.

    At the same time as the base and sides of the **headland** are eroded, weathering will attack the top of the headland. A combination of these two processes will lead to the roof of the **arch** eventually collapsing, leaving what is known as a **stack**. **Abrasion** will erode the base of the stack making it more unstable until it may be knocked down, usually in storm conditions by large waves, leaving behind a **stump**.

4. Longshore drift causes pebbles and sand to be moved along the coast in the direction of the prevailing wind.

    Pebbles and sand are deposited in the mouth of the river to create a sandbank called a spit.

    Slow-moving river water causes deposition and the formation of marshland behind the spit.

    Hook develops on end of spit if wind blows from opposite direction to prevailing wind.

5.

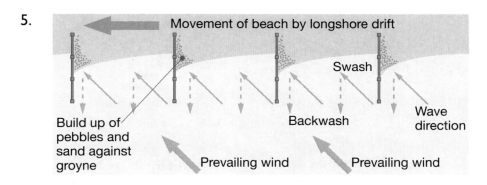

The groynes prevent the pebbles and sand being transported right down the beach.

Exercise 2F

1. The fetch is the distance a wave travels before it breaks on the shore. The more sea or ocean a wave has to travel across as it is blown by the wind the more powerful it can be. The fetch is greatest in Britain on the south-west coast of Cornwall which faces the Atlantic Ocean and its prevailing winds. The opposite end of the southern coast, the south-eastern coast (around Dover in Kent) is exposed to a sea with a fetch that is a mere 40km or so from the northern coast of France. Consequently, the energy and power of the waves hitting the south-western coast are likely to be much higher than are experienced along the south-eastern coast.

2. Various types of weathering may well assist the collapse of an arch as it is eroded beneath by the sea. If it is made of soft rock, the arch could be broken down by chemical weathering. Biological weathering could also contribute to the collapse of an arch if sufficient vegetation grows on top of it.

3. (a) A spit will only form when longshore drift is transporting material from the beach down the coast into the river mouth in the direction of the prevailing wind. Often, the prevailing wind will not direct material into a river mouth and therefore a spit will not form.

    (b) A hook is formed on the end of a spit when the prevailing wind is reversed for a significant amount of time, causing the deposited material to shift in the other direction.

    (c) On the side of the river estuary where the spit has formed, the river water will slow considerably causing significant deposition. This deposited material builds up to create marshland. Marshland cannot be built upon by humans and is therefore left as an undeveloped area, which provides a sheltered habitat for birds and other wildlife.

4. *The coastline of Britain has always looked the same.*

The key points that should be made are as follows:
- longshore drift has caused deposition to build up areas of land that were once in the sea (e.g. Romney Marsh in Kent)
- coastal erosion in areas of predominately soft rock has caused areas that were formerly coastal strips of land to disappear into the sea (e.g. Holderness in Yorkshire)
- in areas where there is significant fetch and a variation of rock type, coastal features such as headlands and bays, and associated headland features such as arches and stacks have developed (e.g. Swanage in Dorset)

Nothing can be done to prevent the loss of coastal settlements due to erosion.

The key points that should be made are as follows:
- groynes can be used to prevent longshore drift removing beaches (e.g. Bournemouth in Dorset)
- concrete sea walls can be built in front of cliffs composed of less resistant rock in order to prevent erosion (e.g. Dover in Kent)
- sea walls can be reinforced by rock armour (e.g. Holderness in Yorkshire)
- expensive coastal defences such as groynes, sea walls and rock armour only slow down coastal erosion and will never totally prevent it

Exercise 2G

1. Landslides can occur when the rock and soil that makes up the slope can no longer support its own weight. The weight a slope bears is often made worse by human activity such as building or farming in terraces. However, extra weight and an increased slope angle alone do not cause landslides. Landslides are triggered by the soil and underlying rock becoming saturated after heavy rainfall. **Saturated rock** bears a lot of weight. This makes it unstable and, with the water acting as a lubricant, rock and soil can slide downhill.

Landslides do occur naturally when steep slopes become saturated but they are becoming more frequent in areas where humans are building on **unstable steep slopes. Human intervention** is a common problem in LEDCs where poorer people are forced to live in unplanned, unregulated shanty towns within cities.

2. Multiple answers are possible but all answers should emphasise the sudden horror that was unleashed on the community by means of reference to the extracts in the textbook (Figs. 2.4.2 and 2.4.3).

3. Answers could include the following facts:
   - One of the worst landslides to occur in Britain took place in Aberfan in Wales on 21st October 1966.
   - Aberfan is a small village in South Wales.
   - Many of the residents worked in the coal mine near the village.
   - After coal is extracted from the ground, a large amount of waste material and rock is left behind. For many years this waste material and rock had been piled up in between the coal mine and the village of Aberfan in large mounds called spoil heaps.
   - In the years and months leading up to 21st October 1966, local residents, the district council and the National Union of Mineworkers had all expressed concerns that these spoil heaps may become unstable.
   - The National Coal Board, which was in charge of the mine, ignored these safety fears and allowed the mine to continue building up the spoil heaps.
   - Heavy rainfall saturated the permeable rock beneath the spoil heap resulting in a small spring pouring water out directly underneath the spoil heap. The spring lubricated the spoil heap and a landslide followed at 9:15am on 21st October sweeping into the village.
   - The primary school was engulfed killing 116 children.
   - The landslide also killed 28 adults.

4. (a) **Causes of the Mississippi flood**
   Check pupils' star diagram contains the following points:

   Natural:
   - The Mississippi River is nearly 4000 km long and has a drainage basin that covers over 30% of the USA, so it was always liable to flood.
   - It has over a hundred different tributaries feeding water into it including the Missouri, the Ohio, the Tennessee and the Arkansas, all of which are bigger than the Thames in England.
   - Heavy rainfall throughout April and May 1993 led to the drainage basin becoming saturated.
   - This was made worse by thunderstorms increasing in intensity throughout June and July, one giving 180 mm of rain in just a few hours.

Human:

- To stop flooding of farmland and cities along the Mississippi, the American government had strengthened the natural levees along the Mississippi throughout the 20th century. This meant that the river was unable to flood and river levels had continued to rise well above the level of the floodplain.

(b) **Effects of the Mississippi flood**

Check pupils' star diagram contains the following points:

Immediate:

- Levees collapsed due to the pressure of the water and the floodplain was flooded up to a width of 25 km.
- In all, an area bigger than Britain was covered in water.
- River traffic was halted; roads and railways were closed.
- In all, 43 people died; 50 000 homes were destroyed; 70 000 people were evacuated.

Long-term:

- The water took months to drain off the land and not only was the 1993 crop destroyed but farmers were unable to plant crops for the following year as the ground was too wet.
- Stagnant water and sewage led to disease.
- The clear-up operation to salvage properties took months.
- The overall cost to the economy of the USA was estimated at £8 billion.

5. Pupils could use any of the following examples to explain one method that has been adopted to overcome future flooding on the Mississippi. Check any diagrams that have been drawn.

Diversionary spillways are gaps in the levees which are deliberately created to allow the river to flood at given points along its course. This allows the river to flood naturally but in places where people do not build or farm.

Dams and reservoirs built on the tributaries of the Mississippi allow the control of water flowing into the Mississippi thus, when river levels are high, water can be kept back safely in the reservoirs.

Tree planting (**afforestation**) in the valleys of the Mississippi's tributaries increases the water which is absorbed naturally in the drainage basin, and therefore reduces the amount of water flowing into the Mississippi. This is a natural and cheap solution but takes a long time to be effective.

Levees have been further strengthened especially around towns and cities. This would not work on its own and contributed to the flood in 1993, but can be effective when combined with the other three methods.

6. Multiple answers are possible, for example:
   - Nether Burrow (6175) because it is on the floodplain at the confluence of two rivers.
   - Melling (5971) because it is built on the edge of the floodplain and has several small tributaries coursing through it which could overflow during periods of intense precipitation.

Exercise 2H

1. Landslides are more likely to occur in LEDCs because poorer people are forced to live in unplanned unregulated shanty towns on the outskirts of cities.

   If the outskirts of these cities are surrounded by steep slopes they may become unstable with the weight of the shanty towns particularly when heavy rainfall saturates the underlying rock.

2. Check any diagram that has been drawn.

   One of the worst landslides to occur in Britain took place in Aberfan, a small village in South Wales, on 21st October 1966. The landslide was the result of a spoil heap collapsing and sliding down on to the mining village below. When the coal from the nearby mine was extracted from the ground, a large amount of waste material and rock was left behind in large mounds called spoil heaps. The waste material and rock was piled up in between the coal mine and the village of Aberfan over many years. Heavy rainfall in the winter of 1966 saturated the permeable rock beneath the spoil heap nearest to Aberfan resulting in a small spring emerging from underneath the spoil heap. The spring lubricated the spoil heap and a landslide followed.

   The National Coal Board was held responsible for this tragedy and, after investigation, was forced to pay compensation to the victims' families. For years and months leading up to 21st October 1966, local residents, the district council and the National Union of Mineworkers had all expressed concerns that these spoil heaps might become unstable. The National Coal Board, which was in charge of the mine, ignored these safety fears and allowed the mine to continue building up the spoil heaps.

3. The Mississippi has always been a high-flood-risk river because of its size. It is nearly 4000 km long, has a drainage basin that covers over 30% of the USA and has over 100 tributaries feeding it such as the Missouri, the Ohio, the Tennessee and the Arkansas, all of which are bigger than the Thames in England.

4. Human intervention unintentionally increased the flood risk on the Mississippi. In the decades leading up to the 1993 flood, the natural levees along the Mississippi were reinforced with concrete, creating artificially high banks. For example, the levees at St Louis had been built up to a height of nearly 16 metres. This meant that the river was unable to flood, and river levels had continued to rise well above the level of the floodplain. This human influence combined with the natural influences caused the flood in 1993.

5. There have been some advantages and some disadvantages in the building of dams on the tributaries of the Mississippi. The advantages have been that the dams have allowed the water authorities to regulate the flow of water into the Mississippi. Therefore, to prevent the Mississippi flooding when it is high, they can hold back water from tributaries such as the Missouri, the Ohio, the Tennessee and the Arkansas in reservoirs.

    The disadvantage of building dams and reservoirs is the expense. There is the cost of building the dam wall, and the cost of buying the land which will be flooded to create the reservoir.

Exercise 2I: Enquiry suggestion
Practical

Exercise 2J: Past exam questions
1. (a) Freeze-thaw weathering.

    (b) Weathering is the breakdown of rock by the weather in one place. Erosion is the wearing away and movement of rock by a force (wind, sea, rivers, etc.)

    (c) Erosion: stack / waterfall
        Deposition: floodplain / beach

2.

River cliff created by erosion

Slip-off slope created by deposition

Fastest flow on outside of river bend

3. (a)   Cliffs

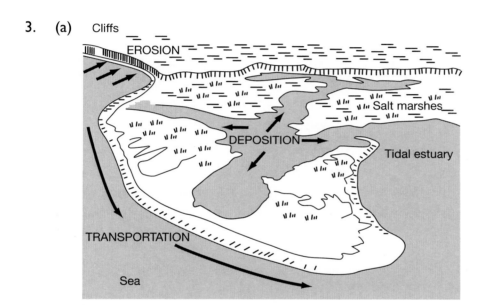

EROSION

Salt marshes

DEPOSITION

Tidal estuary

TRANSPORTATION

Sea

(b) This spit has formed because longshore drift is transporting material eroded from the cliffs along the coast into the river mouth in the direction of the prevailing wind. On the river estuary side of the spit, the river water has slowed considerably causing significant deposition. This deposited material has built up to create the salt marshes labelled. This spit has a hook on it because the prevailing wind here must be reversed for a significant amount of time causing the deposited material to shift in the other direction.

4.

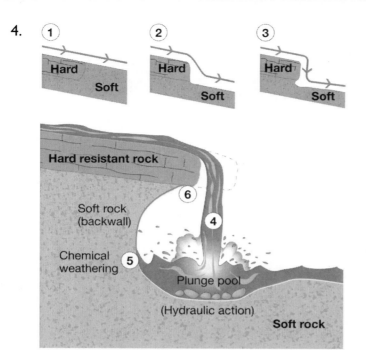

If a river in highland flows over an area where soft and hard rock meet, the softer less resistant rock will erode more quickly. Due to the different speeds of erosion a small thin layer step will eventually form. Eventually the step will be significant enough for the water to begin falling on the lower level of the soft rock (1–3).

The river falling onto the lower level of soft rock will carve out a plunge pool through hydraulic action and possibly abrasion (4).

Spray hitting the soft rock at the back wall of the waterfall will also break down by chemical weathering (5).

As the back wall recedes a larger and larger section of harder, resistant rock will overhang the waterfall.

5. **Levees**, artificially raised banks, can protect land either side of the river from flooding and have been built extensively in urban areas that are situated on floodplains.

Diversionary spillways are gaps in a river's levees deliberately created, to allow the river to flood at given points along its course. This allows the river to flood naturally but in a place where the people do not build or farm.

Dams and reservoirs can be built on the tributaries of a river. These allow the control of water flowing into the main river; when river levels are high, water can be kept back safely in the reservoirs.

Tree planting in a river valley (**afforestation**) increases the water absorbed naturally in the drainage basin and therefore reduces the amount of water flowing into the river. This is a natural and cheap solution but takes a long time to be effective.

Coastal flooding can be limited by the installation of coastal defences such as **rock armour** and **sea walls**.

Exercise 2K: Scholarship or more advanced question

(a)   This answer should make mention of coastal erosion in areas such as Holderness where there is the danger of properties located close to the edge of undercut cliffs falling into the sea, as well as general rock fall and the instability of coastal pathways.

Further to this, candidates may discuss other threats such as storm surges giving rise to coastal flooding (e.g. New Orleans, 2005) and coastal currents.

(b)   Two of the following explanations should be chosen and could be supported by example areas known to the candidate.

Hydraulic action: This is the sheer force of waves hitting exposed cliffs. Air trapped within tiny cracks in the cliff face will be compressed, forcing the rock to weaken and break up upon repetition. The larger the waves, the stronger the effect of the hydraulic action.

Abrasion: Just as a river picks up pebbles and throws them against its bed and banks, the sea picks up pebbles from the sea floor and beaches and throws them against exposed cliff faces. This erodes the cliffs at their base, creating a line that is known as a wave-cut notch. Cliffs collapse over time due to this abrasion and due to weathering on their tops.

Attrition: Pebbles from the sea floor and beach constantly collide with each other as the action of waves breaking on the shore causes them to move forward and back over one another. The pebbles become smaller and rounder due to attrition, ultimately turning into sand. This is similar to the process that takes place in a river's load.

Corrosion: If the cliffs that form the coastline are made of soft rock they may be gradually dissolved as the seawater spray reacts with the rock after a wave has hit them.

(c) This answer should discuss the process of erosion and deposition that are continually at work, meaning that the coast is constantly changing and thus difficult to stabilise. Examples of coastal erosion and spit formation as a result of the processes of longshore drift could be discussed (e.g. Spurn Head). Undercutting, leading to the loss of coastline at places such as Holderness, and deposition, leading to an increase in land at places such as Rye, are facts that may also be incorporated into the answer.

Exercise 2L: Landform processes summary crossword

Answers across:
1. Deposition
2. Gorge
3. Scree
4. Delta
5. Headland

Answers down:
1. Weathering
2. Beach
3. Saturated
4. Load
5. Permeable

Chapter 3: Weather and climate

Exercise 3A

1.

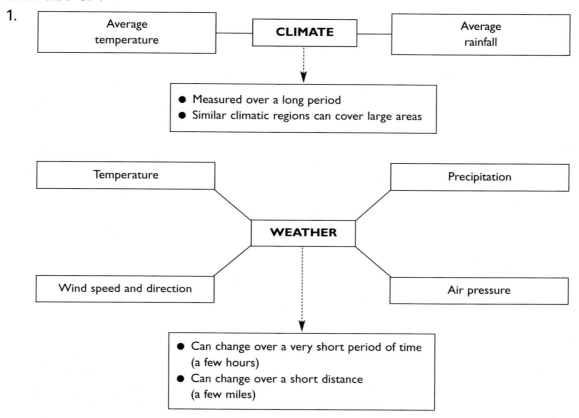

2. A Stevenson's screen is a free-standing weather station that is designed to house meteorological instruments. Within the Stevenson's Screen you would expect to find a maximum/minimum thermometer (which measures the temperature range at the weather station over a 24-hour period) and a barometer (which measures air pressure). By the side of the Stevenson's Screen, you may find an anemometer (which measures wind speed) and a rain gauge (which measures precipitation).

3. Britain receives so much rainfall because for over 80% of the time the wind blows in from the south-west. The winds which influence the weather in an area are called air masses. An air mass is a large body of air, which gets its temperature and moisture levels from its source regions, which are usually flat areas of water or land. The prevailing westerly wind brings the polar maritime and tropical maritime air masses to Britain, ensuring that most of the time the air mass has travelled over the ocean and therefore contains a lot of moisture. The first land the mass encounters is Ireland and then Britain where the moisture is deposited.

4. (a) Evaporation is when water is turned from a liquid into a gas (water vapour) due to heating by the sun.

   (b) Transpiration is when water from plants and trees is evaporated from their leaves.

   (c) Condensation is when cooling causes water vapour to change from its gas state to liquid to form clouds and water droplets.

   (d) Precipitation is water falling to the ground once the clouds have cooled to a point where they can no longer hold their moisture. Precipitation can take the form of rain, snow, sleet and hail.

5. Microclimate is the term that describes slight differences in temperature and precipitation within a small area from its surrounding area. There are various factors that can influence these differences in temperature and rainfall. Buildings can influence microclimate in several ways.
   - In Britain, south-facing sides of buildings are likely to be warmer than northern sides which will be in the **shade**. A building that faces south (has a southerly **aspect**) will experience a warming effect.
   - Another influencing factor can be the **prevailing wind**. Because the prevailing wind in Britain is from the west, the west sides of buildings tend to receive more precipitation and feel cooler, while east-facing sides of buildings may be **sheltered** and feel warmer. If passages between buildings are in line with the prevailing wind, **wind channelling** can occur, causing such passages to feel cold and gusty.
   - The immediate surroundings of buildings may be a few degrees warmer than other outside areas in **winter** because heat escapes from buildings that are centrally heated.
   - Darker **surfaces**, such as tarmac, absorb heat and will therefore be warmer than lighter surfaces that reflect heat, such as grass, especially on a sunny day.

Exercise 3B

1. When isobars are spread apart on a weather map it means that pressure is high and winds are very light. The weather will therefore be stable with clear skies, making it cold and crisp in winter and warm in summer. The air mass that is most likely to bring such conditions to Britain would be the tropical continental air mass.

2. Rocks that can absorb water and allow water to move within them are called **permeable** rocks. After precipitation, water soaks into permeable rock and begins to flow back to the river or sea through the rock as groundwater. Tree

roots may penetrate the permeable rock as well as the overlying soil and absorb groundwater, a process called **interception**, which then leads to transpiration from the leaves of the trees. If the underlying rock is impermeable (cannot absorb water), tree roots can only intercept water flowing through the soil not the rock, therefore levels of interception, and therefore transpiration, are lower.

3. The answer may include reference to buildings and their aspect, road/playground surfaces; natural influences such as the relief of the land, trees and so on.

4. The answer should state that Britain's weather is influenced by a wide variety of factors including air masses and microclimate. The answer then should discuss how these two factors can lead to a wide variety of weather conditions that change by location and over relatively short periods of time. Other factors may be discussed such as relief, latitude and distance from the sea. These factors combine to make Britain's weather very unpredictable and changeable, and therefore often the topic of conversation.

Exercise 3C

1. (a) Britain's climate is temperate.

    (b) Britain generally experiences warm summers and mild winters, with rainfall occurring throughout the year.

    (c) We find temperate climates in areas of the globe far away from Britain such as New Zealand because both countries are at the same line of latitude, albeit in different hemispheres. Climate bands are related to the latitude of a region and can occur at the same latitudes in either hemisphere, therefore a temperate climate can be found in the northern hemisphere between 40 and 60 degrees north (Britain) and in the southern hemisphere between 40 and 60 degrees south (New Zealand).

2. It is generally a few degrees warmer in the south of Britain than in the north of Britain in the summer because the south receives the sun's rays at a more direct angle. The sun's rays travel at a wider angle to reach the north of Britain. They therefore have to travel through more atmosphere where they lose some of their strength.

3. (a) Fig 3.2.3 shows us that, in winter, it is warmer in the south west of Britain than it is in the north and north east of Britain. For example, in January, the average temperature in Cornwall is 7°C whereas it is only 4°C in Newcastle and eastern coastal regions of Scotland.

(b) If I decided to go for a swim in the sea on Christmas Day, I would choose the south-west coast because the water temperature there would be several degrees warmer than at the east coast due to the warming influence of the Gulf Stream.

4. It is drier in the east of Britain than the west because the prevailing wind comes from the south-west. This means that most of the time, the air has to travel over the west before it arrives at the east. Much of the moisture carried by the air masses will be dropped on the higher relief in the west, over mountain ranges such as Snowdonia and the Lake District, and so often the winds are drier by the time they reach the east.

5. (a) Singapore's climate is equatorial.

(b) Pupils should present the following information in the form of a star diagram.

Singapore's equatorial climate
Singapore's equatorial climate is warm and wet throughout the year with high levels of humidity.

Factors that influence Singapore's climate:
- **Latitude** – just 2° north of the equator means Singapore receives constant direct overhead heating from the sun throughout the year, giving a temperature of around 27°C every day.
- **Surrounded by sea** – Singapore is on a peninsula therefore is surrounded by sea. The constant heat from the sun evaporates the sea water and causes convectional rainfall to occur over Singapore on a daily basis. Also the warmth of the sea acts as an insulator for the peninsula that Singapore is located upon, never allowing the land to cool down.
- **Prevailing winds** – convectional rainfall is added to by rain brought by monsoon winds in November and January.

Exercise 3D
1. The coldest and wettest places in Britain occur where the relief is high, particularly in the north and on the west coast of Britain. Examples are mountain ranges such as the North West Highlands in Scotland, the Lake District in Cumbria and Snowdonia in North Wales, which receives over 1500 mm of rainfall on an annual basis (see Fig. 3.2.4). These locations will be cold because they are areas of high land but will also be very wet because they are the first landmasses to receive the moist westerly and northerly winds.

2. Humidity is the level of moisture in the air. When humidity is high the air feels warm and sticky. Singapore always has a high level of humidity because moisture from the surrounding sea evaporates into the air due to the constant overhead heating by the sun.

3. The sea influences Britain's temperate climate in two ways. The south-west of Britain is warmer in winter than the north and east because of the warming influence of the Gulf Stream. This warm current of water runs from the Gulf of Mexico to the south-west of Britain and raises sea temperatures and consequently land temperatures by several degrees. The sea also influences precipitation. One of the reasons why the west of Britain receives more rainfall than the east is because the prevailing south-westerly winds pick up moisture from the Atlantic Ocean and also the Irish Sea before depositing it on mountains such as those in the Lake District and Snowdonia.

    The sea also has an important role in shaping Singapore's equatorial climate. The sea holds its temperature for a longer period of time than the land. In Singapore the sea never cools because it is always receiving heat from the direct overhead sun, which means that the sea acts like an insulator to the Singapore peninsular and maintains the temperature of the land at an average of 27°C. The sea is also the reason why rainfall is so high in Singapore. The sun evaporates moisture from the sea and releases it over the land as convectional rainfall.

Exercise 3E

1. (a) An anticyclone in February would give very cold, clear and still weather.

    (b) A depression in March would give mild but wet and windy weather.

    (c) An anticyclone in August would give very hot, clear and still weather.

2. The Lake District is a mountain range on the west coast of Britain in Cumbria. It receives a lot of rainfall because it is the first landmass that **the prevailing south-westerly winds** meet after they have picked up a lot of moisture from the Atlantic Ocean and Irish Sea. This moist air is soon forced to rise rapidly over the mountains of the Lake District after it reaches the west coast of Cumbria, causing **condensation** and then precipitation over the Lake District; this is a process known as relief rainfall. After much of the moisture has been released as rain or snow, the air descends on the eastern side of the Lake District and warms in an area known as the rainshadow.

3. **Warm and cold air masses meet in the Atlantic Ocean**

A boundary between the two air masses is formed.
This is called a front.

The warm air rises over the cold air along the front.

The warm air cools by around 1°C for every 100 metres it rises,
and condenses to form clouds.

The warm air continues to rise, cool and condense
leading to precipitation along the front.

4.

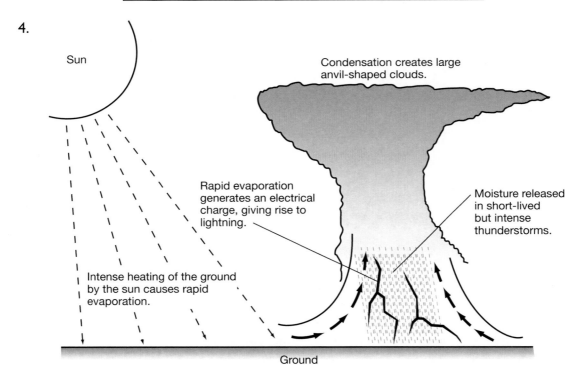

Sun

Condensation creates large
anvil-shaped clouds.

Rapid evaporation
generates an electrical
charge, giving rise to
lightning.

Moisture released
in short-lived
but intense
thunderstorms.

Intense heating of the ground
by the sun causes rapid
evaporation.

Ground

Exercise 3F

1. If the isobars on a weather map of Britain were close together this would
    suggest that pressure was low, giving strong winds and suggesting that Britain
    would be experiencing a depression. However, if the isobars were spread further
    apart this would indicate pressure was high, giving light winds and suggesting
    Britain would be experiencing an anticyclone.

2. (a) Cockermouth would regularly receive relief rainfall because it is located on the western side of the Lake District mountain range. Moist westerly winds will condense and precipitate over the mountains around Cockermouth.

(b) Dubwath may receive convectional rainfall on a hot August day as it is located very close to a lake. When the high pressure of an anticyclone is dominating, water will be evaporated from this lake and this could lead to a sudden and intense downpour, as associated with convectional rainfall.

(c) Cockermouth is one place in Britain that is likely to receive all three types of rainfall: convectional, relief and frontal. It is located in the north of Britain on the west coast and is one of the first landmasses to receive frontal rainfall from any depressions moving in from the Atlantic Ocean. The high relief of the Lake District means that Cockermouth will also be subject to relief rainfall as the air masses condense and precipitate. Convectional rainfall may also occasionally occur in Cockermouth because it is located near the water masses of the Irish Sea and the lakes of the Lake District, which may evaporate to give rise to convectional rainfall on very hot summer days.

3. Convectional rainfall is rare in Britain because it only occurs when temperatures are very high and there is sufficient water to be evaporated. It only happens occasionally on hot summer days. However, along the Equator, temperatures are constantly high due to the overhead heating of the sun and many places are surrounded by sea water (e.g. Singapore) or large rivers (e.g. the Amazon) which can be evaporated to give convectional rainfall.

Exercise 3G

1. (a) Global warming is the artificial heating of the Earth's atmosphere caused by heat from the sun's rays being trapped by a layer of carbon dioxide.

(b) Governments can reduce global warming by developing renewable sources of energy such as hydroelectric, wind, geothermal, tidal, wave or solar power, or invest in nuclear power rather than relying on non-renewable sources of energy that burn fossil fuels such as coal and oil. Governments could increase taxes on flying to discourage the use of aircraft, which emit large amounts of carbon dioxide. Individuals can help reduce carbon emissions by limiting the use and number of their cars and saving energy in their homes, for example by turning off unnecessary lights.

2. Hurricanes only occur above warm areas of oceans, such as the Gulf of Mexico. In order to form, hurricanes need a source of very warm, moist air derived from tropical oceans with surface temperatures greater than 27°C.

3.

Late August 2004	A tropical storm developed in the north-west Atlantic Ocean. As it moved in a westerly direction and gained strength it was soon upgraded and given the name of Hurricane Frances.
2nd September	Many institutions closed.
3rd September	Poulation of Florida evacuated the area.
4th September	Hurricane Frances began to batter the east coast of Florida in the USA. It picked up speed and ferocity, dropping over 15 cm of rain in a 24-hour period, lashing the coast with wind speeds reaching in excess of 230 km per hour.
8th September	Damage to property widespread.
13th September	Power restored.

4. Multiple answers are possible but pupils should attempt to empathise with the feelings of those affected by Hurricane Frances. The account should indicate that wind speeds and rainfall increased significantly but then calmed temporarily while the eye of the hurricane passed, followed finally by another increase in destructive winds and heavy rainfall.

Exercise 3H

1. Reducing carbon dioxide emissions is the responsibility of both individual people and organisations. Major organisations such as the UN and EU have an important role in implementing policies that will limit industrial emissions of carbon dioxide as do multi-national companies, some of whom are encouraging environmentally irresponsible development in countries such as China. However, individuals should also take a role in trying to reduce their carbon footprint by switching to energy-saving domestic appliances and using public transport.

2. Climatic change is a real and significant phenomenon. Higher atmospheric temperatures are leading to the rapid melting of the ice caps and result in many glaciers retreating. This in turn is causing rising sea levels and therefore increases the frequency of coastal flooding. Rising atmospheric temperatures mean that sea and land temperatures are also rising rapidly. This can cause land and marine

vegetation to die and therefore upsets food chains, habitats and whole ecosystems. Changes in atmospheric temperatures are also seen as the cause of more intense weather activity.

The cause of climate change has been directly related to increased emissions of carbon dioxide as a result of industrial and domestic energy use. However, it must be said there has been some degree of over-exaggeration and manipulation of scientific data by the media which has sensationalised the global warming phenomenon. This does not mean it is not real and action at all levels must be taken.

3. Individuals should adopt the following precautions and procedures to limit the damage and risk to life hurricanes can cause:
    - evacuating in line with weather-forecast warnings
    - securing property by boarding up windows
    - turning off electricity and gas supplies
    - putting sandbags outside property to reduce risk of flooding

4. Global warming is increasing sea temperatures. This has resulted in an increase in the number of hurricanes developing in the Gulf of Mexico during one season.

Exercise 3I: Enquiry suggestion
Practical

Exercise 3J: Past exam question
1. (a) Microclimate is the term that describes slight changes in temperature and precipitation within a small area.

    (b) (i)   Aspect of buildings
        (ii) Colour of surface
        (iii) Shelter from prevailing wind

2. (a) (i)   A
        (ii) B
        (iii) B
        (iv) C

    (b) A will be the warmest location because it receives warm westerly winds and the warming influence of the Gulf Stream.

    (c) B will be wettest because it is the highest point. Warm wet air blown from the west will condense and precipitate over point B, giving relief rainfall.

3. (i) y
   (ii) x
   (iii) x
   (iv) z
   (v) x

4. **Convectional rainfall** occurs mainly in the east of Britain because this is where temperatures are highest on sunny days in the summer, leading to convectional rainfall. There is also plenty of surface water to be evaporated in East Anglia, particularly in the Norfolk Broads National Park.

   Frontal rainfall develops in the Atlantic Ocean to the west of Britain where warm and cold air masses meet. As the warm air rises over the cold air it cools, condenses and brings rain along a line called a front. The front will sweep across Britain in a south-easterly direction, bringing rain to all parts.

   Relief rainfall is caused by warm wet air being forced to rise over hills or mountains. When it does so, the moisture condenses and then precipitates. Most hills and mountains in Britain are in the north or west of Britain such as Snowdonia or the Lake District.

5. (a) (ii)
   (b) (iii)
   (c) (ii)
   (d) (iii)

Exercise 3K: Scholarship/more advanced question

Pupils' answers should demonstrate their knowledge of the wide variety of variables that can influence the weather (air masses, microclimate, weather systems – anticyclones and depressions) and make Britain's weather, in reality, unpredictable. A strong answer will discuss the methods by which the weather is recorded and the simplification of this data into manageable weather charts that the public will understand. Further to this, example areas should be referred to where possible.

Exercise 3L: Weather and climate summary crossword

Answers across:
1. Meteorologist
2. Latitude
3. Buildings
4. Humidity
5. Microclimate

Answers down:
1. Mild
2. Isotherm
3. Beaufort
4. Air mass
5. Transfer

Chapter 4: Settlement

Exercise 4A

1. Nomadic tribes in Britain 10 000 years ago decided to settle in one place because they learnt how to grow crops from seed and rear animals, rather than just collecting wild vegetation and hunting wild animals. To grow crops and rear animals they needed to live in one place, thus settlements began.

2. Surplus is the word used to describe the extra produce a farmer might produce. If a farmer creates an excess he may choose to trade it with other nearby settlements.

3. Sheffield has grown into a large city today as it has many important site and situation factors. It has a water supply in the River Don. It has high ground which will have been useful for defence. It has a series of bridging points. It is a natural route centre located at the head of three valleys – the River Don, River Loxley and River Riveline. The floodplain of the River Don will have provided excellent farmland, although it has now been developed and there are woodlands surrounding Sheffield.

4. Oughtibridge has not grown in the same way as Sheffield because, although it has some important site factors such as a bridging point, a route centre and a river, its growth has been severely limited by the steep valley sides that surround it.

5. Multiple answers are possible. For example, pupils may choose Kirkby Lonsdale, which has the following important original site factors:
   - close to water supply
   - bridging point
   - route centre
   - on higher relief away from floodplain

Exercise 4B

1. Tribes learnt to grow crops and rear animals for their own needs instead of hunting wild animals and gathering food growing in the wild. This meant that they could stay in one place and settle.

2. If a farmer produced too much food for his family to consume he might choose to sell this surplus. To sell it, he would have to meet people from different settlements at a convenient point, often a route centre or bridging point.

3. The situation of a settlement is important in determining whether it has the potential to grow. Settlements that have good situation factors may grow. For

example, Sheffield was originally surrounded by woodland and fertile farming land. Other settlements are limited by their situation. For example, Oughtibridge near Sheffield has not grown because steep valley slopes surround it.

4. At first glance settlements may appear to be randomly scattered on the landscape but this is not true. There is always a physical reason why an area may have few or many settlements, why settlements vary in shape and why some settlements are larger than others. For example areas of high relief, such as the Lake District, will have fewer and smaller settlements in a dispersed pattern because the land limits their number and size whereas an area of flat land with good communications, such as south-east England, has a much greater density of settlements including large towns and cities that have benefited from positive site and situation factors and therefore have grown.

Exercise 4C

1. **A nucleated settlement**

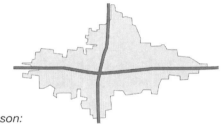

Reason:
• Crossroads • Market place • Castle at centre
• Bridging point/ford • Village green
• River confluence • Cathedral at centre

A linear settlement

Reason:
• Road between two larger settlements • River
• Valley bottom • Coast/large lake frontage

A dispersed settlement

Reason:
• Farmland • High relief
• Physical landscape (forest/lakes/desert)

2. **Nucleated settlements** are built around a central point such as a river confluence, a bridging point or ford, a castle, a cathedral or a market place.

    Linear settlements are built in a line shape and can be found along major roads between larger settlements, along the coastline, tracking the valley floor or around the edges of large lakes.

    Dispersed settlements are small and spread out because the land is needed for farming or for physical reasons such as the land being mountainous, densely forested, covered in lakes or desert.

3. The functions of a settlement are the reasons why it has grown and the purpose of the settlement: the things that happen there. Functions include commercial, residential, administrative, industrial, tourism and services.

4. Check that the pupils have identified the correct functions of their local town or city and that they have given appropriate evidence to support their answers.

5. Commercial   –   stadium (3788)
    Residential   –   Longley estate (3591)
    Industrial   –   works (3291)
    Tourism   –   information centre (3587)
    Services   –   hospital (3690)

Exercise 4D

1. Check pupils have chosen an example of a linear settlement from the OS map extract of Sheffield, and that they have drawn a sketch of it including details such as buildings, roads, rivers and contour lines. Check also that the sketch has a clear title.

    One example they might have chosen is Oughtibridge:

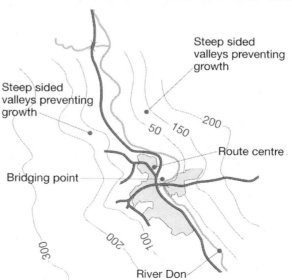

2. Check pupils have correctly identified dispersed settlements and given the correct six-figure grid reference. Check that they have given reasons why the settlements are dispersed and that they have quoted map evidence in their answers.

   One example they may have chosen is Storrs (293893). This settlement is dispersed due to its high relief and because the surrounding land is probably farmland.

3. As settlements grow, their functions change and usually increase in number. London has all six different functions today but originally began as a trading settlement on the Thames, with a residential and commercial function. As the city grew it would have developed an administrative function and provided services for its population. The Industrial Revolution in the 19th century would have meant that London would have developed an industrial function followed closely by a more modern and increasingly important tourism function.

Exercise 4E

1. Pupils should have drawn a pyramid (as below) and added to it an example of a hamlet, village, town and city to illustrate the settlement hierarchy of their local area.

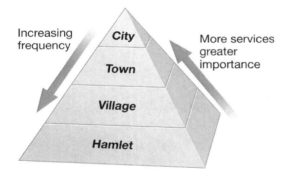

2. Worrall is a village. You can tell it is a village because of the number of buildings and services it has. Worrall has one school, a post office, a church and a public house – the typical services found in a village.

3. You would expect to find convenience goods for sale in Worrall. Because it is a village with a small population, Worrall will have a low threshold and a small range that can only support one or two shops selling convenience goods.

4.

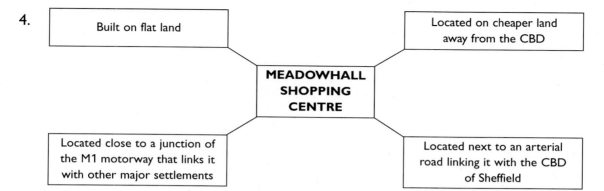

Built on flat land

Located on cheaper land away from the CBD

MEADOWHALL SHOPPING CENTRE

Located close to a junction of the M1 motorway that links it with other major settlements

Located next to an arterial road linking it with the CBD of Sheffield

5. The building of out of town shopping centres in the city suburbs can have tremendous effects on the CBD of the city. The number of shoppers visiting shops in the CBD can fall causing a reduction in the amount of money taken. Many shops are forced to close down. Empty shops can be targeted by vandals making the city centre less attractive, which in turn can deter new businesses from starting up in the CBD.

An example of this can been seen in Sheffield. Since Meadowhall's opening in 1990 it has been reported that takings at shops in Sheffield's CBD have been reduced by 25% and many have been forced to close down.

Exercise 4F

1. Check pupils have allocated the cities, towns, villages and hamlets to the correct levels of their triangular settlement hierarchy of South Yorkshire.

Cities: 1 – Hull.

Towns: 3 – Market Weighton, Beverley, South Cave.

Villages: 6 – Sancton, North Newbald, Little Weighton, Bishop Burton, Cherry Burton, South Dalton.

Hamlets: 10 – North Cliffe, South Cliffe, Everthorpe, High Hunsley, Risby, Eppleworth, Gardham, Arras, South Newbald, Riplingham.

2. 3092 Advantages: Near A6102 for access to catchment area and linking it to the CBD and other areas of the city.

Cheaper land away from city centre.

As a department store offering high order services this would appeal to the surrounding area where possibly only low order services are available.

Disadvantages: Away from busy city centre (CBD).

Uneven land for building.

3990 Advantages: Excellent access via M1, A6102 and A631 for very good access to catchment area and linking it to the CBD and other areas of the city.

Near Meadowhall shopping centre.

Disadvantages: Little land available for building.

Land more expensive at this site.

3587 Advantages: In heart of CBD, near market.

Flat land for development.

Disadvantages: Most expensive land to be developed.

Very little opportunity to build/no room for expansion, little space for parking.

3. Meadowhall shopping centre was built where it was for the following reasons:
- Excellent access via M1, A6102 and A631
- Flat land for development
- Near CBD for market but cheaper as near sewage works
- Surrounded by residential areas which provide labour

388879 would be an example of another suitable site for building an out of town shopping centre for the following reasons:
- Excellent access via A6102 leading to the M1
- Near railway station for public transport access
- Flat land for development
- Near CBD for market but cheaper as near railway line
- Surrounded by residential areas which provide labour

4.

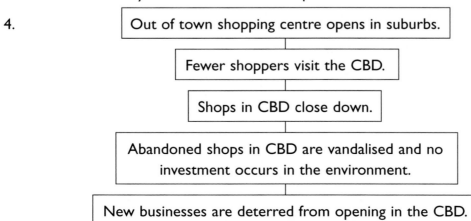

Out of town shopping centre opens in suburbs.

Fewer shoppers visit the CBD.

Shops in CBD close down.

Abandoned shops in CBD are vandalised and no investment occurs in the environment.

New businesses are deterred from opening in the CBD.

Exercise 4G

1. (a) Land use is the term used to describe the way an area of land is utilised. This may be residential, commercial or industrial, or the land may be left undeveloped, for example as parkland.

   (b) A geographical model is a diagram that simplifies and generalises patterns we find in geography. An example of this is a concentric circle model, which generalises land use patterns in cities.

2.

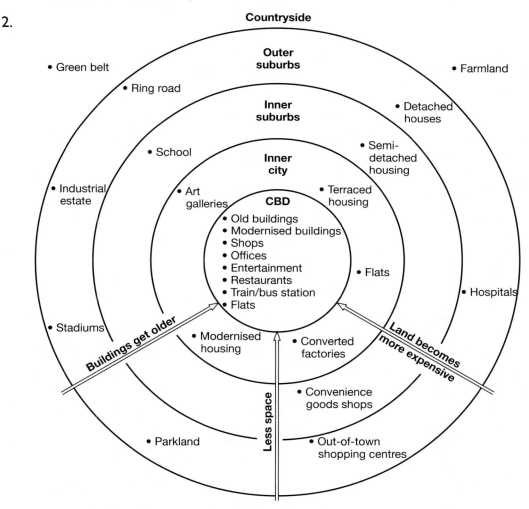

3. The concentric circle model shows us that in a typical city in an MEDC you would expect to find the following:
   - The buildings become newer as you move from the CBD to the outer suburbs, although older buildings in the CBD may have been renovated or may coexist with new office blocks.

- As you move to the outer suburbs, there is likely to be more space and the price of land falls, allowing for larger houses and providing suitable sites for hospitals, universities and other land uses that require cheaper land and a larger site.

4. In the outer suburbs you would expect to find larger detached houses with gardens, but as you move towards the CBD, less space is available and the land becomes more expensive, thus houses become smaller. In the inner suburbs you may find semi-detached housing, with terraced housing dominating the inner city. Not much room is available for housing in the CBD and it is usually limited to apartment blocks.

5. Urban sprawl is the continual outward growth of cities and towns. To prevent cities like London continually growing and taking up the surrounding countryside, the government created green belts to surround these cities. You have to have special planning permission to build within the green belt. In this way urban sprawl is contained.

Exercise 4H

1. Here is an example answer:

There are a variety of different land uses in the **outer suburbs** because there is a lot more space, the land is cheaper and ring roads give good access. Houses in the outer suburbs tend to be large, **detached** and have large gardens. The outer suburbs may also contain sports stadiums, hospitals, universities, council estates, industrial estates and out of town shopping centres.

The **inner suburbs** form the next zone of the city. The land use in the inner suburbs is mostly for housing. The space available means that housing tends to be **semi-detached**, and houses have gardens and garages. This zone tends to have newer, more recently built housing, and will occasionally be accompanied by schools and shops selling **convenience goods**.

Moving towards the CBD, the next zone in the concentric circle model is the **inner city**. Typically you would find **terraced housing** in this zone. These houses are small, arranged in rows and will be old as they were built to accommodate factory workers during the **Industrial Revolution**. Old factories, commonly mills, will have been converted into other land uses such as housing, museums or art galleries.

The **CBD** may contain old buildings as it was the likely starting point of the city but will also have modern buildings and old buildings that have been **modernised**. The CBD will have lots of shops, restaurants and entertainment facilities such as nightclubs and bars. It will also have office blocks, but only a small amount of land use in the CBD will be given to housing which might be in apartment blocks due to the very limited space available. The CBD will be the meeting point for transport in the city so train, bus and tram stations are all located in the CBD.

2. Shopping facilities are found in the CBD because this is the central point of a city where transport systems such as trains and roads meet and where people work. However, out of town shopping centres have developed in the outer suburbs to serve a very large residential market. They have developed here because the land is cheaper and there is room for expansion.

3. Generally, Sheffield does fit into the pattern shown by the concentric circle model. The CBD can be found in grid square 3587 where we can see there is a bus terminal, train terminal, information centre, cathedral, town hall, museum, route centre and many churches. The inner city and inner suburbs are mostly residential, as one would expect.

    However, because Sheffield is built in a valley advantage can be taken of the flat land along the valley floor, hence a lot of the land uses we would expect in the outer suburbs are found nearer to the CBD. For example, we would expect to find the Don Valley Stadium in the outer suburbs but it is in fact located in grid square 3888 just two kilometres from the CBD. In the concentric circle model we would expect this area to be purely residential.

4. Check pupils' reasons for believing whether or not their local town or city fits the concentric circle model.

5. Conurbations are formed as a result of urban sprawl. Examples include Manchester/Liverpool which have grown together to form one large urban area, and Edinburgh, Glasgow and Greater London have all grown outwards. Planning laws such as those protecting the green belt have been introduced to reduce urban sprawl. This aims to limit the development around a city, attempting to prevent its continuous outward growth. New towns like Milton Keynes have been created around London to focus growth elsewhere. National Parks have been created partly to prevent urban sprawl taking hold of the countryside. For example, the Peak District National Park limits the growth of the Manchester conurbation.

Exercise 41

1. **Migration** is the movement of people from one place to another.

   To **emigrate** is to move to a different country.

   An **immigrant** is somebody who has moved to a foreign country from their own country.

   A **refugee** is someone who has been forced to migrate within a country or from one country to another because of a natural disaster, war or unrest.

2. Very poor LEDCs such as Somalia are prone to natural disasters such as drought leading to famine. Faced with such a situation, people have little choice other than to migrate from their homes in order to find food. Unfortunately, many of these poor LEDCs are governed by corrupt or unstable regimes, resulting in war or political oppression offering further reasons for migration.

3. The major driving force behind migration from MEDCs to other MEDCs is employment. Most employment in the target MEDCs is temporary, although an attractive climate and environment may encourage temporary migrants to become permanent migrants. For example, Australia accepts many skilled workers from Britain who want to practise their trade in Australia and enjoy the long-term benefits of a more welcoming climate.

4. **Rural-urban migration** is the re-location of people from the countryside to the city. It occurred in Britain during the Industrial Revolution and is occurring today in LEDCs.

   Counterurbanisation is the process of people moving from cities back to the countryside, and occurs in Britain today due to better transport and communications.

5. Pupils should present the following information in the form of star diagrams.

   Reasons why villages are becoming suburbanised:
   - People want a better environment.
   - Better transport.
   - Development of business parks in rural areas.
   - Rapid improvement in communications.

   Problems of suburbanised villages:
   - Large numbers of commuters who use the services of the town/city where they work, means decreased services in the village through lack of use.

- Older people feel isolated due to lack of transport.
- Young people feel isolated due to lack of transport and services leading to petty crime.

Exercise 4J

1. Illegal immigrants risk the threat of prison to live in a different country than their own for a variety of reasons. They may face extreme poverty in their home country or sometimes it might be political persecution that drives them out.

2. Counterurbanisation is affecting the function of rural settlements. Villages are changing as people decide to leave the cities and live in the countryside. Before counterurbanisation, villages were small in size and population, with residential, service and commercial functions to support them. As people have flooded in, villages have become larger with much higher populations and new housing estates. These villages still, however, only provide a residential function; services have not expanded in the way one might have expected.

3. Check pupils' choice of suburbanised village – multiple answers are possible. For example, they may choose Oughtibridge (3093). A village that becomes suburbanised may have increased numbers of commuters living in the village who use city services. This in turn may cause local shops and services to close down, isolating immobile groups such as the young and elderly.

Exercise 4K: Enquiry suggestion

Practical

Exercise 4L: Questions from past exam papers

1. Settlements in rural areas that are a significant distance from major towns or cities are declining in population. This is because there are few job opportunities for adults in these settlements and it is too far for them to commute to a major town or city. This is true of many settlements in East Anglia and Lincolnshire, both of which rely heavily upon agriculture and there are now fewer people employed in agriculture than previously.

Villages that are within easy and close proximity to large settlements are growing in population as people seek to live in a more rural area away from the dangers and expense of the city, while still commuting to the city for work. While these dormitory settlements may have an increased population, the number of services goes down as most people still use the services of the nearby city. Thorpe Hesley near Sheffield is a good example of this type of settlement.

2. (a) A is located in the CBD.

   B is located in the inner suburbs in a linear fashion along a main road.

   C is located within the residential area of the inner city/inner suburbs.

   D is located on a main road leading to the motorway in the outer suburbs.

   (b) Shopping malls (A) are located in the CBD because this is where the main transport systems meet and thus where most shoppers will be.

   The shopping street (B) will have developed in this location because it is serving the needs of residents in the inner city/outer suburbs but also attracting the custom of commuters using the main road into the city centre.

   Corner shops (C) can be found in the inner suburbs because there is a demand from the local residents for convenience goods to be available locally.

   Large superstores locate in the outer suburbs (D) because the land is cheaper here; there is room for large stores and room for them to expand and good access for residents of the city and surrounding settlements via the motorway and access road.

3. In an MEDC we find the most expensive housing in the outer suburbs, but in LEDCs the outer suburbs often contains shanty-type settlements.

   In an MEDC most industry develops around the ring road in the outer suburbs but in LEDCs it usually develops along the main roads or railway lines leading into the city.

4. Site – within a river meander and built on top of a hill (Castle Hill) which would have provided a good vantage point for defending the town in the past.

5.

A	B
Department store, university, airport	City
Few scattered houses, no shops	Hamlet
Primary school, shop, post office	Village
Secondary school, library, bank	Town

Exercise 4M: Scholarship or more advanced question from a past paper

(a) This answer should define the difference between site and situation (see Glossary), giving examples of important site factors and ideally referring to an example such as Sheffield. Further to this, the answer could explain how a combination of positive site and situation factors may have led certain settlements to grow into the large cities we know today, whereas limitations of physical geography may be the reason why other settlements have remained similar to their original size.

(b) This answer should introduce the idea of counterurbanisation in MEDCs and its causes. An example should be referred to, such as Thorpe Hesley near Sheffield. A strong answer would balance this with a reflection that the opposite is happening in rural areas of LEDCs where **rural-urban migration** is leading to population depletion in rural areas.

(c) This answer should lead on from part (b) by analysing the social issues that counterurbanisation creates in rural communities where the housing increases but services decline due to a higher proportion of the population being commuters and using the services of the city. A strong answer would draw in the concept of range and threshold for village services such as convenience stores and public transport, referring to the example discussed in part (b). Mention should also be made of rural-urban migration in LEDCs leading to the abandonment of farms in rural areas and ageing rural populations.

(d) This is a speculative answer and candidates are advised to use their knowledge as a basis to predict future patterns rather than wildly predicting events that have no geographical background. Examples of past and present patterns are always useful in predicting the future.

Exercise 4N: Settlement summary crossword:

Answers across:
1. Commuter
2. Migration
3. Shanty
4. Rural
5. Detached

Answers down:
1. Modernised
2. Function
3. Urban
4. Nomadic
5. Linear

Chapter 5: Location knowledge

Exercise 5A

1. The seven continents are Africa, Antarctica, Asia, Oceania, Europe, North and South America.

2. A Indian Ocean
   B Arctic Ocean
   C Pacific Ocean
   D Atlantic Ocean
   E Southern Ocean

3. F Cape Horn
   G Cape of Good Hope

Exercise 5B

1. 1 Sahara desert
   2 Mt Kilimanjaro
   3 tropical forest in Brazil
   4 tropical forest in the Democratic Republic of Congo

2. X Mount Everest

3. The Alps are in Europe.
   The Andes are in South America.
   The Himalayas are in Asia.
   The Pyrenees are in Europe.
   The Rockies are in North America.

4. Amazon flows into the Atlantic Ocean.
   Ganges flows into the Indian Ocean.
   Mississippi flows into Gulf of Mexico.
   Nile flows into the Mediterranean Sea.
   Rhine flows into the North Sea.
   Yangtze flows into the Pacific Ocean.

Exercise 5C

1. A Severn
   B Trent
   C Thames

2.   A Belfast
      B Dublin
      C London

3.   Line Y

Exercise 5D
1.   D Manchester
      E Edinburgh
      F Cardiff
      G Glasgow
      H Birmingham

2.   (a) 1
      (b) The Republic of Ireland (Eire)

3.   V Lake District National Park
      W Pennines

4.   Peak District National Park and Yorkshire Dales National Park

Exercise 5E
1.   A Spain
      B Germany
      C Italy
      D Russia
      E Greece

2.   A Madrid
      B Berlin
      C Rome
      D Moscow
      E Athens

3.   Y

Exercise 5F
1.   (a) Poland
      (b) Warsaw
      (c) 2

2. France, Switzerland, Austria, Hungary, Romania

3. Paris, Bern, Vienna, Budapest, Bucharest

4. (a) Morocco
   (b) USA and its capital Washington DC
   (c) Canada and Mexico

Exercise 5G

1. (a) The Tropic of Capricorn
   (b) 23.5° south

2. (a) The Antarctic Circle
   (b) 66.5° south

3. (a) The Prime Meridian
   (b) 0 degrees

Exercise 5H

1. (a) Washington DC
   (b) Los Angeles

2. (a) Sao Paulo
   (b) Rio de Janeiro

3. (a) Mumbai
   (b) New Delhi

Exercise 5I

Practical

Exercise 5J: Questions from past papers

1. A Cairo
   B Paris
   C San Francisco
   D Madrid

2. X The Peak District
   Y The Lake District

3. (a) Check pupil's answers
   (b) Check pupil's answers
   (c) Check pupil's answers

4.   L Democratic Republic of Congo
     M Brazil

Exercise 5K: Location knowledge summary crossword

Answers across:

1.   Amsterdam
2.   Shannon
3.   Andes
4.   Everest
5.   Mozambique

Answers down:

1.   Himalayas
2.   Nile
3.   Delhi
4.   Manchester
5.   Mississippi